PRESCHOOL CHR
VALUE LESSONS

by
Kathy Darling

illustrated by Darcy Tom

Cover by Jeff Van Kanegan

Shining Star Publications, Copyright © 1991
A Division of Good Apple

ISBN No. 0-86653-627-2

Standardized Subject Code TA ac

Printing No. 98

Shining Star
A Division of Frank Schaffer Publications, Inc.
23740 Hawthorne Boulevard, Torrance, CA 90505-5927

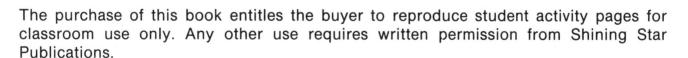

Unless otherwise indicated, the New International Version of the Bible was used in preparing the activities in this book.

DEDICATION

To Bruce, Luke, and Wendy

May we continue to grow in His gifts.
I love you.

SS1891

INTRODUCTION

Preschool Christian Value Lessons offers parents and teachers a unique opportunity to nurture the spiritual awakening of toddlers and preschoolers. Designed especially for three- to six-year-olds, this book is brimming with fun, creative ways to introduce young children to the general meanings and common symbols associated with the fruit of the Spirit.

Through these age-specific activities you will help children build a value base that they can proudly embrace. A scriptural passage is offered at the top of each page as an inspiration to you as well as the children. Each chapter starts with a coloring page, then goes on to gifts that the children make themselves, songs, simple recipes, games, action verses, activities, and crafts. Each chapter ends with a special Tabletop Tots section that offers easy solutions for learning centers. Finally, the last page in each chapter offers a list of resources that can be used to complement the lessons.

Some activities need more adult involvement than others, but please always supervise while allowing children to grow in their independence and creativity. Get to know your group before you begin; there is a wide range of abilities within a group of very young three-year-olds and more worldly four-year-olds. Scissor skills may not yet have been mastered by some children, resulting in occasional frustration. Also, be wary of some of the materials used. A young three-year-old who is still prone to tasting everything may not be ready to work with buttons or sequins. For this child, collecting interesting objects on a nature walk might be too dangerous an activity to attempt just yet.

As Christian preschool educators, you play an important role in the lives of the young children you teach. Thank you for being where you are, for taking the time to share your life and your energy with the children of our world. You are feeding the hearts and souls of our future. So get out the paint, the glue and the glitter, tune up the old guitar, and have fun!

TABLE OF CONTENTS

Love   Joy   Peace   Gentleness   Faithfulness   Goodness   Patience   Kindness   Self-Control

LOVE

"But the fruit of the Spirit is love, . . ."   Galatians 5:22

LOVE POSTER

Children can cut out the picture and color it. They may glue the picture to colored construction paper. Save all the posters to make a fruit of the Spirit banner later. Valentine's Day is a special day for showing our love. Let the children think of other ways in which they can say "I love you" daily.

                    SS1891

A GIFT OF LOVE: PAGE SAVER

Materials:

One-inch wooden hearts in different colors, 6- to 8-inch lengths or longer of one-inch wide ribbon, scissors, glue (Check your local craft store for the pre-painted wooden hearts and craft ribbon for pennies a yard. If wooden hearts are not available, simply glue together two heart shapes cut from felt.)

Instructions:

Let children choose the color of heart and type of ribbon they wish to use. Then have them spread the last inch of the top side of the ribbon with glue. Press on the heart and let dry completely. Children may give this gift of love to their favorite bookworms.

A GIFT OF LOVE: SWEET DREAM SACHET

Materials:

8- or 9-inch squares of colorful fabric, pipe cleaners or ribbons, potpourri mixture, artificial flowers

Instructions:

Cut the pipe cleaners in half. Have the children place the fabric squares on the table, right side down. Pour a tablespoon or two of the potpourri mixture into the center of the fabric. Gather up the edges of the fabric to the center, and secure by twisting a pipe cleaner or ribbon around it. Place an artificial flower at the center and twist again to close completely.

Let the children give this Sweet Dream Sachet to a loved one to be placed near her pillow until bedtime. Encourage the children to say a special prayer for that person at bedtime. Always remove the sachets from beds at night or naptime.

"...live a life of love, just as Christ loved us and gave himself up for us..."

Ephesians 5:2

TROUBLES DON'T BOTHER ME

Sung to: "Shoo Fly, Don't Bother Me"

Troubles don't bother me, worries don't bother me.

Troubles don't bother me, for I belong to somebody!

When I am feeling sad, when I am feeling blue,

When I am feeling bad, I know that I can turn to You!

I know, I know, I know that I'm loved by Him!

I know, I know, I know that He cares for me!

Troubles don't bother me, worries don't bother me.

Troubles don't bother me, for I belong to somebody!

When I am feeling sad, when I am feeling blue,

When I am feeling bad, I know that I can turn to You!

SS1891

"...I will walk in my house with blameless heart." Psalm 101:2

RECIPE FOR LOVE: ALMOST HOMEMADE HEART COOKIES

This activity lets the children get right down to the fun part—cutting, baking, and sampling! Put the finished cookies on small paper plates, cover, tie with a bow, and add a small note: "Health Information: Made with Real Love."

Materials:

Heart-shaped cookie cutters, cookie sheets, spatula

Ingredients:

1 pkg. refrigerator roll sugar cookies, 1/3 cup powdered sugar, 1 Tbs. flour, red confectioner's sparkles

Instructions:

Chill dough well as directed on the package. Mix the sugar and flour, and use half to coat the work surface. Take half the cookie roll and coat the sides with the sugar mixture. (Keep other half in refrigerator until needed.) Roll out dough to about 1/8 inch thick. Dip the cutters in sugar, then let the children press the heart cutters firmly but carefully into the dough. Lift with spatula onto ungreased cookie sheet and bake at 350 degrees for 7 to 9 minutes. Remove and let children sprinkle on liberal amounts of red confectioner's sparkles.

                                                    SS1891

"This is the message you heard from the beginning: We should love one another."

I John 3:11

TELEPHONE FOR LOVE GAME

Materials:

Red construction paper, marker, basket

Instructions:

Cut out a red paper heart for each person. Mark each with a child's name. Put the hearts in a basket and sit in a circle. Hold the basket and start the game by pulling out a heart. Read the name on the heart silently and then place the heart in your pocket. Starting to your right, whisper something nice about the person on the heart. Always start with the person's name, like "John shares well" or "Suzie tells fun stories." The message should be whispered from one to another all around the circle, until it returns to you. The last person repeats the message out loud. Tell what the real message was, if needed. The person on your right now draws a heart, reads it silently, hides it, and play begins again. Play until something nice has been whispered about everyone. If a child draws his own name, he should return it and draw again.

SS1891

" 'Love the Lord your God with all your heart and with all your soul and with all your mind and with all your strength.' "

Mark 12:30

THIS HEART O' MINE ACTION VERSE

The Lord gave us sunshine,
(Open fingers like a sunburst.)

And skies of brilliant blue.
(Put hands over eyes, then point to sky.)

The Lord made this heart o' mine
(Place hands over heart.)

Full of love for you!
(Outstretch arms, then point to listener.)

LOVE BIRDS ACTION VERSE

This is a Love Nest,
(Intertwine fingers to make a cup.)

These are the Love Birds!
(Place thumbs together, spread fingers and wiggle like feathers.)

Love is the sweetest word
(Place hands over heart, tilt head, blink eyes up and down.)

I have ever heard!
(Put hand to ear.)

SS1891

"Dear friends, since God so loved us, we also ought to love one another."   I John 4:11

LOVE PUPPETS

Materials:

White paper lunch bags; red markers or crayons; sequins, buttons or other decorative items for eyes; pink felt scraps; glue

Instructions:

Place the paper bag flap side up. Consult the diagram and outline a large heart shape onto the bag. Cut small half circles from the felt scraps. Have the children color the heart with red markers or crayons. They should also lift up the flap and color the bag red underneath. Glue on two sequin or button eyes. Glue on the half circle just under the flap so that a little is visible. This forms a mouth. When the children are finished decorating their Love Puppets, encourage them to try them on and get them talking. Love Puppets are special because they only talk when they have something nice to say! Love Puppets can be used at home to tell everyone that they are loved and are very special people.

I love your bedtime stories!

You give great hugs!

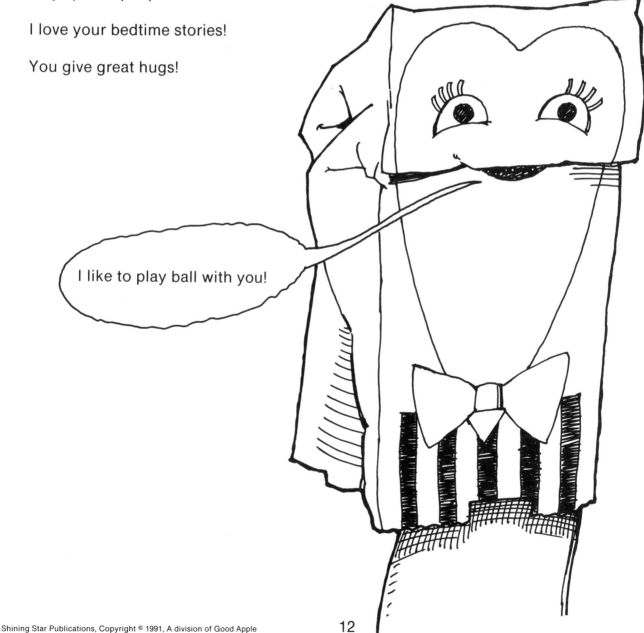

I like to play ball with you!

"Children, obey your parents in everything, for this pleases the Lord."   Colossians 3:20

TREE OF LOVE

Materials:

Brown and green construction paper, scissors, glue, star stickers, photos of each child's family and friends

Instructions:

Show the children how to fold a sheet of green construction paper in half lengthwise and then make cuts in and out to form a Christmas tree shape. Using brown construction paper, cut out and glue on a small tree trunk at the bottom. Use scissors to trim the photos into interesting shapes, or simply cut out around the faces of family and friends. Glue the photos onto the tree like ornaments. Press on some sparkly stars. Write "Tree of Love" and the child's name at the top.

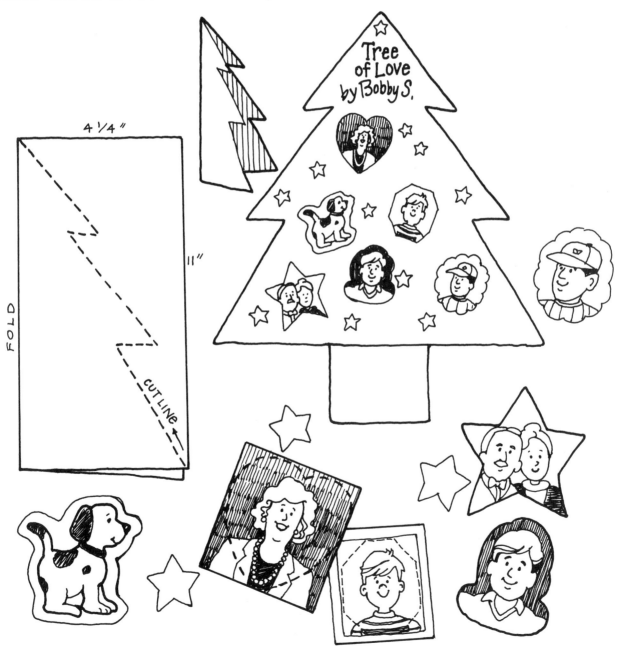

Shining Star Publications, Copyright © 1991, A division of Good Apple   SS1891

"... 'Love your neighbor as yourself.' "   Matthew 22:39

LOVE SHIRT: ONE SIZE FITS ALL

Materials:

Plain brown grocery bags, scissors, stickers, brushes and red paint or red markers or crayons

Instructions:

Place the folded bag before you as in diagram #1. Fold the bottom flap up as in diagram #2. Cut into the bag to create a heart shape as follows: Cut a V into the top of the bag, being sure to cut through all layers of the fold. This will be the neck hole. Then cut the bottom of the bag into the pointed shape of the heart. (See diagram #3.) Have the child pull the bag over his head, mark for arm holes and cut. After it is on, you may wish to trim the bag near the sides of the neck so the paper does not bother the child. Doing so will not alter the heart shape.

After the bag is cut, allow the children to decorate their Love Shirts in any way they wish. They may want to paint them entirely red or use crayons and stickers to make them into giant, wearable Valentines!

"Dear friends, let us love one another, . . ." I John 4:7

TABLETOP TOTS: LEARNING CENTER SOLUTIONS
HEART SIZING

Materials:

Different fabric scraps or several colors of construction paper, black construction paper, scissors, glue

Instructions:

Cut the fabric or colored paper into heart shapes of five distinct sizes, ranging from very small to large. Divide them into five piles of different-sized hearts. Line up the five hearts in a row and glue to a large sheet of black construction paper. Start with the smallest and end with the largest. Label the card with the child's name. Valentine's Day can come at any time of the year! Have the children give their cards to a special friend as an expression of their love.

          SS1891

RESOURCES

Ideas for speakers, field trips, projects, books, and other supplementary materials and activities.

Invite a florist to speak to the children. A flower arranger helps others to send out their messages of love. Ask the florist to talk about how her own feelings are expressed in the arrangements that she creates. Many people send flowers on Valentine's Day. Remind the children that we like to send our love on many other occasions, too. Ask them to think of others: a baby is born, a person is sick, a loved one dies, a friend is going on a trip, a birthday, a job well done, or just because!

Bring in some flowers and ferns and small, clean, empty glass jars. Let the children try flower arranging. Encourage them to work slowly and create something they really feel shows their love.

Try the following books and tapes at circle time to share with your group:

Brown, Margaret Wise
The Runaway Bunny
Harper and Row Publishers Inc., 1942.
The heart-warming tale of a mother's enduring love.

Minarik, Else Homelund
A Kiss for Little Bear
Harper and Row Publishers Inc., 1968.
Love is infectious, as a kiss is passed along from messenger to messenger.

Munsch, Robert
Love You Forever
Firefly Books, Ltd., 1986.
The constancy of love through generations shown beautifully and humorously.

Williams, Margery
The Velveteen Rabbit, music cassette
Random House, Inc., 1985.
A classic, with Meryl Streep narrating and George Winston on piano.
Dancing Cat Records, Box 639, Santa Cruz, CA 95061

Hostvedt, Jan
Loving Somebody
Chariot Books, a division of David C. Cook Publishing Co., 1985.
Bible quotes on loving and caring.

JOY

"and my spirit rejoices in God my Savior,"   Luke 1:47

JOY POSTER

Children can cut out the picture and color it. They may glue the picture to colored construction paper. Save all the posters to make a fruit of the Spirit banner later. Have the children think of many situations that fill them with joy: special holidays, birthdays, family outings, hearing a good joke, having a favorite dessert. Remind them it is fun to spread their joy around, simply by expressing what they are feeling.

SS1891

"I have much to write to you, . . .so that our joy may be complete."   II John 12

A GIFT OF JOY: A FANCY FLIGHT

Materials:

Large balloons, sheets of paper, ribbon, crayons, helium tank

Instructions:

Contact your local party store and inquire about helium tank rentals. It is usually a nominal charge. Have the children draw colorful, joyful pictures on their papers. Older children may wish to write a simple, joyful message like "Peace on Earth" or "Share the Joy." Help the children fold and then roll their pictures up tightly so they may be inserted into the balloons. Fill the balloons with helium, tie with ribbon, and then release them, sending messages destined to find their way into someone's field, backyard, or schoolyard. This colorful surprise will certainly spread joy when discovered.

Read this rhyme together, before releasing the balloons:

Balloon! Balloon! On a fancy flight!
Thank you, God, for colors bright!

Balloon! Balloon! A colorful toy!
Fly away and bring some joy!

"Sing to him a new song; play skillfully, and shout for joy."   Psalm 33:3

PASS THAT JOY AROUND

Sung to: "It Ain't Gonna Rain No More"

Pass that joy around, around,
Pass that joy around!
God above, He sends His love,
So pass that joy around!

Pass that joy around, around,
Pass that joy around!
Just sing His song all day long,
And pass that joy around!

Pass that joy around, around,
Pass that joy around!
God above, He sends His love,
So pass that joy around!

SS1891

"When they saw the star, they were overjoyed."   Matthew 2:10

RECIPE FOR JOY: SHINING STAR SANDWICHES

Materials:

Star-shaped metal cookie cutter, paper plates, plastic knives

Ingredients:

Whole wheat or white sandwich bread, American cheese slices, sandwich spreads

Instructions:

Let the children cover their slices of bread with their favorite spreads. Lay the bread and the cheese on a cutting board. Show the children how to press the cookie cutter quickly and firmly into the bread and then the cheese. Lift up carefully. If necessary, trim with a knife. Have the children place their star-shaped cheese on their star-shaped bread slice to create a shining sandwich of joy! (Use bread scraps to feed local wild birds.)

SS1891

"But the angel said to them, 'Do not be afraid. I bring you good news of great joy. . .'"

Luke 2:10

FULL OF JOY ACTION VERSE

Joy at Christmas when Christ was born.
(Cradle baby in arms.)

Beat your drum, blow your horn!
(Pretend to blow horn.)

Joy at Easter when Christ arose.
(Crouch on the floor then jump high.)

Feel alive right to your toes!
(Wiggle toes.)

Joy in my heart, full of love.
(Place hands over heart.)

Praise our Lord high above!
(Clap twice, throw arms up.)

THE JOYFUL BUMP ACTION VERSE

I have joy in my fingers,
(Hold up hands, wiggle fingers.)

And joy in my toes.
(Point to toes and wiggle them.)

I've got joy in my heart,
(Point to self.)

And here it goes!
(Nod twice.)

Bump! Bump! Bump! Bump!
(Thump chest four times.)

JOY RIDE

Materials:

White paper plates, paper lunch bags, crayons, stapler, lightweight cardboard, glue

Instructions:

Have the children create paper plate steering wheels by coloring in a horn at the center of the plate and then adding any other details they choose. Staple one edge of an open lunch bag to the bottom of the steering wheel. Go for a joy ride to your favorite park, beach or stream, or through your own backyard. Have the children make loud revving noises as they steer their cars along the path as you lead them.

Ride around in joy marvelling at God's gifts of nature. Let the children pick up anything interesting and deposit it in the bag. They might pick up twigs, small pebbles, pretty pods or seeds, leaves, flowers, etc. When you return, make a joyful collage. Glue everything on cardboard to make a pretty design. IMPORTANT: Always be aware of toxic plant life. Many common backyard plants are toxic if eaten or handled improperly. Consult a guidebook if you are not familiar with poisonous plants in your area.

Staple edge of bag to bottom of plate.

"...that I may be filled with joy."   II Timothy 1:4

JOY IN DOING GAME

KEEPING COMMANDMENTS: KEEP THE SABBATH HOLY

Discuss this commandment. Encourage the children to think of active ways it can be fulfilled.

Materials:

Construction paper, markers, multi-colored star stickers, bulletin board or papered wall area

Instructions:

Make a simple sketch of a church on construction paper and tack it to the board. Let the children approach the bulletin board one by one and press on a star sticker. Ask the children to name the ways that they are able to keep the Sabbath, the most special and holy day of the week. Attending church service is an obvious answer, but ask them to think about the other special things they can do to honor this day. Perhaps there are little rituals that their families take part in to foster closeness, like Sunday drives, pancake breakfasts, or picnics. Or maybe they do other things that help to spread the love of Christ, like visiting elderly relatives or doing favors for friends.

                                SS1891

"...you...are filled with an inexpressible and glorious joy," I Peter 1:8

BLUEBIRD OF HAPPINESS

Materials:

Toilet paper tube, blue construction paper, scissors, glue, blue glitter

Instructions:

Make two short slits opposite one another on one end of the tube. Outline the bluebird pattern (see next page) on the blue paper. Have the children cut it out, or do this for them if they are unable. Make a few lines of glue all over the tubes, and then shake on some blue glitter. Let dry a moment and shake off the excess. Gently slide the paper bird into the slit to create the Bluebird of Happiness.

Show the children how the wings flap if they gently wiggle the tube up and down. Let the children give this Bluebird of Happiness to someone they love in order to spread some joy.

Shining Star Publications, Copyright © 1991, A division of Good Apple

SS1891

Bluebird pattern

SS1891

"...remain in my love, ...that your joy may be complete."   John 15:10,11

STAR LIGHT, STAR BRIGHT

Materials:

Yellow construction paper, multicolored star stickers, glue, glitter, hole punch, yarn, scissors

Instructions:

Make a copy of the star pattern on yellow paper. Have the children connect the dots, then cut it out. Let them press a gummed star onto each point of the star or decorate in any way they wish with the glitter and glue. Make a hole with a hole punch and string with yarn. Have the children hang the stars in their bedroom windows to remind them to be joyful each new day.

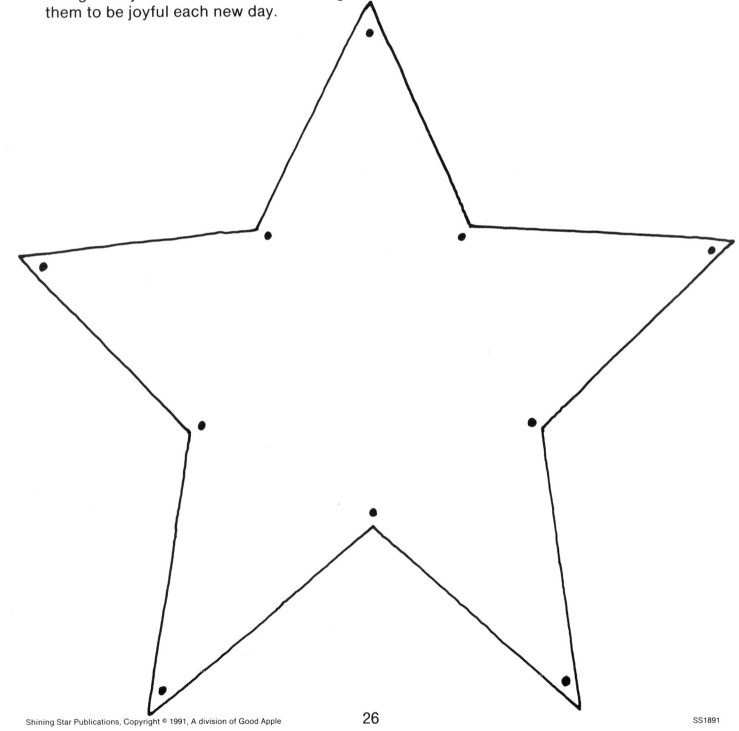

SS1891

"If you obey my commands, you will remain in my love, . . . that my joy may be in you and that your joy may be complete." John 15:10, 11

TABLETOP TOTS: LEARNING CENTER SOLUTIONS
JOY STICKS

Materials:

Popsicle sticks, circles of colored construction paper, sequins, Q-tips, glue, markers or crayons

Instructions:

Make one Joy Stick as a sample and place it on the table. Glue one end of the Popsicle stick between two circles of paper. Let dry a few minutes. Create happy faces by first dipping the Q-tip in glue, dropping two spots of glue onto the paper circle, and pressing on sequins for eyes. Draw in a huge smile. Let dry a few minutes. Let each child make several Joy Sticks so that he can surprise someone who looks like she needs a lift. Joy Sticks can be dropped into a favorite coffee cup or pencil holder, stuck between the pages of a book, or slipped into a pocket! It's a great way to lend a smile!

Glue stick in between paper.

SS1891

RESOURCES

Ideas for speakers, field trips, projects, books, tapes, and other supplementary materials and activities.

Invite a performing artist to share his talents and speak to the children. A dancer or singer could vividly portray the importance of sharing one's joy in life. Ask the guest to speak specifically about the importance of entertainers in our daily lives and how it feels to entertain and make others happy.

Try the following books and tapes at circle time to share with your group:

Anderson, Debby
God Is the Greatest
Chariot Books, a division of David C. Cook Publishing Co., 1985.
A wonderful book for use with young children.

Carlson, Nancy
I Like Me
Viking Penguin, Inc., 1988.
This little pig's joyfulness starts with being happy with herself.

Staines, Bill
All God's Critters Got a Place in the Choir
E. P. Dutton, 1989.
All God's critters make a joyful noise in this fun book.

Thigpen, Thomas Paul
Come Sing God's Song
Chariot Books, a division of David C. Cook Publishing Co., 1987.
Joyous book of praise and thankfulness; vibrant illustrations.

SS1891

PEACE

"If it is possible, as far as it depends on you, live at peace with everyone."

Romans 12:18

PEACE POSTER

Children can cut out the picture and color it. They may glue the picture to colored construction paper. Save all the posters to make a fruit of the Spirit banner later. Ask the children what types of behavior at home help them keep the peace among their family members. Sharing? Respect for privacy? Thoughtfulness?

SS1891

A GIFT OF PEACE: HOME ORNAMENT

Materials:

9″ x 12″ sheet of black construction paper, four Popsicle sticks, red paper, scissors, glue, yarn, hole punch

Instructions:

Cut the sheet of black paper in half so it measures 9″ x 6″. Cut a small heart from the red paper. Show the children how to glue the four Popsicle sticks onto the black paper in the shape of a house. Glue the red heart inside the house. Make a hole with a hole punch at the top, string with yarn, and let the children hang this above the doorway to their homes as a symbol wishing "Peace be to this house."

". . .live in peace. And the God of love and peace will be with you."

II Corinthians 13:11

I AIN'T GONNA FIGHT NO MORE

Sung to: "It Ain't Gonna Rain No More"

I ain't gonna fight no more, no more.
I ain't gonna fight no more.
When I play, I'll share my toy,
I ain't gonna fight no more!

I ain't gonna push no more, no more.
I ain't gonna push no more.
When I play, I'll take my turn,
I ain't gonna push no more!

I ain't gonna grab no more, no more.
I ain't gonna grab no more.
When I play, I'll be polite,
I ain't gonna grab no more!

Help me play, my Lord, my Lord.
Help me play, my Lord.
Teach me how to be a friend,
And I'll have fun, my Lord.

SS1891

"Make every effort to keep the unity of the Spirit through the bond of peace."

Ephesians 4:3

RECIPE FOR PEACE: SWEET DOVE OF PEACE

Materials:

2 round cake layer pans, knife, large serving tray, green paper, scissors

Ingredients:

1 package of white cake mix, one 1-pound tub of ready-to-serve white frosting, confectioner's decorative silver balls, lifesaver or round candy piece for eye

Instructions:

Bake the cake as directed in two round layers. Let cool completely. Place one layer on the center of the serving tray for the body of the dove. Frost. Carefully slice evenly across the other layer so that it is flat on both sides. Following the diagram, carefully cut this round into the four pieces as shown. Place the wing pieces on top of the first layer as shown and frost. Place the tail and head pieces against the first layer as shown and frost. (Place the four pieces cut side down, so you do not have a problem with loose crumbs when frosting.) Drop silver balls all around the body of the dove, outlining the details. Position the candy "eye." Cut a small olive branch from the green paper and attach to the beak. Admire your creation for a few minutes, say a prayer for peace, and then gobble it up!

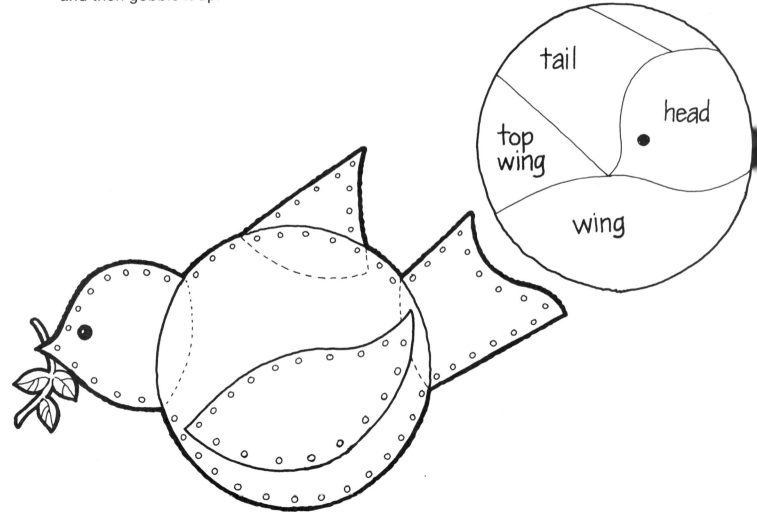

"But the fruit of the Spirit is. . .peace, . . ." Galatians 5:22

PEACE AROUND THE WORLD GAME

Join hands in a circle and play this sing-song game just as you would the more familiar "Ring Around the Rosie."

Peace around the world,

Our hearts full of kindness,

Caring, caring

We all jump for joy!

SS1891

"May the God of hope fill you with all joy and peace. . ." Romans 15:13

PEACE TRAIN ACTION VERSE

The conductor calls,
(Put hand to mouth.)

"Come on, you all!"
(Wave arm to come along.)

Take a ride on the Peace Train!
(Yell, "Toot! Toot!", pull whistle.)

The conductor calls,
(Put hand to mouth.)

"Be a friend to all!"
(Put out hand, shake up and down.)

Take a ride on the Peace Train!
(Yell, "Toot! Toot", pull whistle.)

SS1891

"Let the peace of Christ rule in your hearts, . . ."   Colossians 3:15

WORLD PEACE EXPRESS

Materials:

Several grocery boxes of various sizes (large enough for at least one child to sit in and larger if you can find them); old paper maps of the world, suitable for cutting; butcher paper or newsprint; red paper; strips of burlap or other heavy fabric; scissors; glue; stapler or staple gun

Instructions:

Remove the lids and bottoms from the boxes. If desired, cover the boxes with the butcher paper or newsprint before decorating. Now the children can decorate each of the passenger cars for their World Peace Express. Cut out the shapes of countries or continents from the old maps and glue them onto the cars. Cut several red hearts from the paper and glue them on as well. Connect the "cars" by stapling on the strips of burlap or other fabric to link them.

Let the children pile inside and go for a rollicking ride on the World Peace Express. This is a great time to try out the Peace Train action verse!

"Let us therefore make every effort to do what leads to peace. . ." Romans 14:19

PEACE AT THE END OF THE RAINBOW

This time, not a pot of gold, but peace is at the end of the rainbow—a reminder of what the world really needs now! Let the children trace with their pencils along the path until they find peace at the end of the rainbow. After they have discovered the correct path, let them color it like a rainbow.

SS1891

TABLETOP TOTS: LEARNING CENTER SOLUTIONS
BEANED CROSS

Materials:

Four different types of dried beans or peas with four distinct colors, (try lentils, split peas, black beans, or red kidney beans) cardboard, glue, black marker

Instructions:

On the cardboard, outline the cross with heavy black marker. Separate the four types of beans into dishes. Now let the children spread liberal amounts of glue on each section of the cross. Try to keep the beans off the black outline. Let them fill in each section of the cross with a different color bean or pea. Let dry completely, then display.

RESOURCES

Ideas for speakers, field trips, projects, books, and other supplementary materials and activities.

Invite a representative from the Peace Corps or other humanitarian group to come and share her experiences with the children. Someone who could offer an insight into the children of another country, their hopes, dreams, and their play and work times, would be especially effective.

Try the following books and tapes at circle time to share with your group:

Eco, Umberto
The Bomb and the General
Harcourt Brace Jovanovich, Inc., 1989.
This is an excellent book about peace. It begins with the atoms who, wishing not be used for war, escape from the bomb in order to make it useless. This book may be too involved for use with the youngest children, but is such a good book that it is worth a look for use with 6- and 7-year-olds.

Murphy, Elspeth Campbell
God Cares When I'm Being Punished
Chariot Books, a division of David C. Cook Publishing Co., 1987.
Children will know that God cares for them even in the midst of trouble.

GENTLENESS

". . .the fruit of the Spirit is. . . gentleness. . ."

Galatians 5:22, 23

GENTLENESS POSTER

Children can cut out the picture and color it. They may glue the picture to colored construction paper. Save all the posters to make a fruit of the Spirit banner later. Let the children think of other creatures that we must treat gently, such as a caterpillar or a kitten.

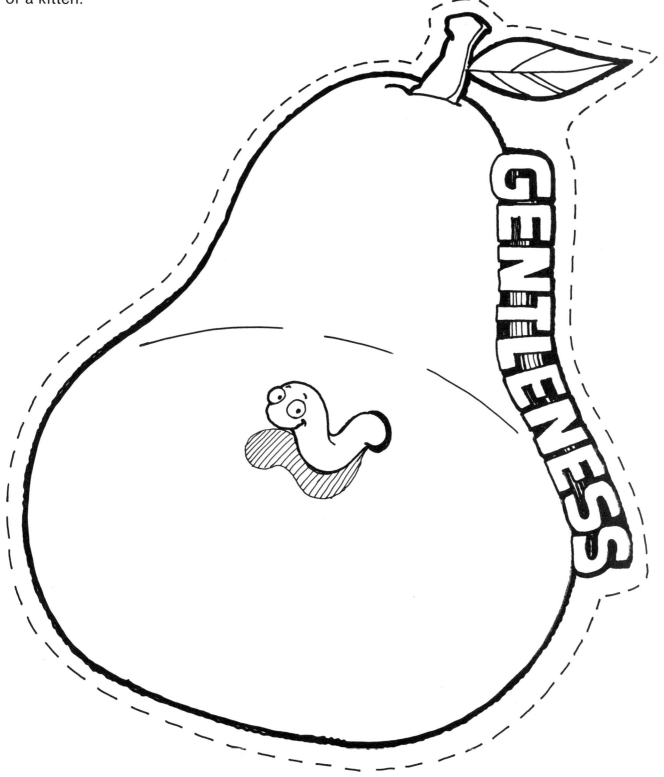

SS1891

A GIFT OF GENTLENESS: EGG VASES

Materials:

Eggs, cardboard egg carton, small colorful craft feathers or straw flowers

Instructions:

Wash each egg carefully in warm water and dry. Make two small holes at the ends of the egg. Blow out the egg to empty it. (Do not let the children put their mouths against the egg as there could be salmonella bacteria on the shells.) Make the hole at the narrow end of the egg larger, not quite as big as a dime. Rinse the inside of the egg with warm water and let dry. Carefully cut the egg carton into sections and trim around to make an even edge. Give each child an egg and a section from the egg carton. Drop a small amount of glue into the carton section and then *carefully* set the egg in the section with the narrow end of the egg and larger hole up. Allow the children to select several of the feathers or flowers and very *gently* place them into their fragile vases.

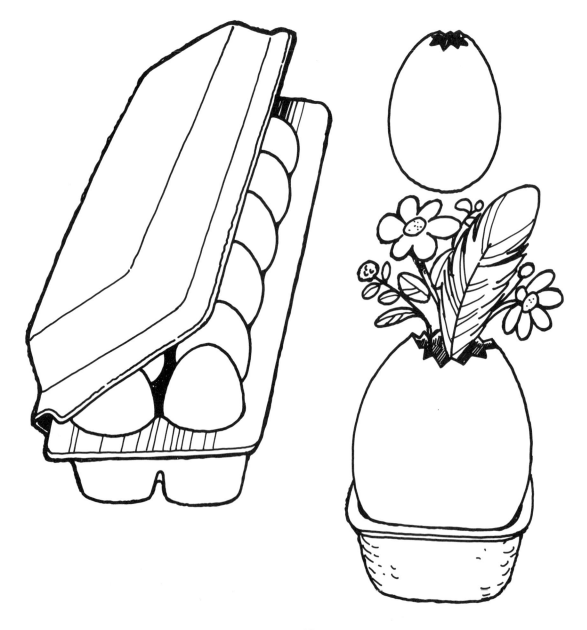

"And he took the children in his arms, . . ."   Mark 10:16

ROCK-A-BYE BABY

(Traditional)

Rock-a-bye, baby, in the tree top,

When the wind blows, the cradle will rock.

When the bow breaks, the cradle will fall,

And down will come baby,

Cradle and all!

But down, down below, waits Mama, so dear.

With open arms, she'll catch you, no fear.

With hugs and kisses, she'll hold you so near,

To love you and keep you,

Sweet baby, dear!

SS1891

"The poor will eat and be satisfied; . . ." Psalm 22:26

RECIPE FOR GENTLENESS: BERRIES ON A CLOUD

Materials:

Paper plates, plastic forks, large spoon

Ingredients:

Packaged ready-made individual shortcakes, Cool Whip or other whipped topping, miniature marshmallows, strawberries or raspberries

Instructions:

Very gently wash and drain the berries. Place a shortcake on each child's plate. Spoon on Cool Whip. Add berries and marshmallows to create Berries on a Cloud.

As the children drop their berries and marshmallows onto the Cool Whip, they can recite the following rhyme:

Little berry, oh, so red,

It's raining gently on your head!

Puffy clouds, floating high,

Softly raining from the sky!

Little berry, growing sweet,

Be my tasty, juicy treat!

  SS1891

"For the Lord takes delight in his people; he crowns the humble with salvation."

Psalm 149:4

GENTLE GIANTS GAME

Play this fun version of 7-Up with a large group of children on a rainy day or any day!

Instructions:

Seven children are initially chosen to be "it" and start the game. They move to the front of the room. All other children sit with their backs to the seven and hide their eyes. The group of seven yells this line before play begins, "Fee! Fi! Fo! Fum! I've got love and want to give you some!" Now the seven walk silently and softly out among the other children. Each one chooses a child, comes up from behind, and gives a gentle hug. Then the seven return to the front of the room, and the hugged children try to guess who did the hugging. If they guess correctly, they get to take the hugger's spot up front and play continues.

During the game, each seated child who has not received a hug holds one thumb up as he sits with his eyes closed. Anyone who receives a hug puts his thumb down. As you supervise the game, be sure to watch that everyone gets hugged by a Gentle Giant at least once before play ends.

 SS1891

"In meekness. . ." II Timothy 2:25 (KJV)

GENTLENESS ACTION VERSE

I'm quiet as a caterpillar,
(Wriggle silently on the floor.)

Mild as a mouse.
(Put up ears.)

I'm gentle as a lamb.
(Baaa baaaa.)

Soft as a kitten.
(Meeoow.)

I'm tender as a teddy bear,
(Hug self, rock back and forth.)

Warm as a bunny.
(Hold up paws and hop.)

I'm cuddly and so full of love,
Pucker up, I'll give you some!
(Throw a kiss to the crowd.)

 SS1891

"I have set you an example that you should do as I have done for you."   John 13:15

GENTLE GESTURES

Christ showed great gentleness when he washed the feet of his disciples. Let children know that it is all right to show gentle acts of affection toward one another. Set aside a quiet time to show each other some gentleness.

Materials:

Have each child bring his own hair brush and a small pillow.

Instructions:

Give the children a chance to show some gentle care for one another. Have children lie down in stocking feet with their heads on small pillows. Let them take turns rubbing one another's feet.

Choose partners or make a train with children sitting on the floor one behind the other. Have the children gently brush a friend's hair, taking care not to tug or pull. (For health reasons, make sure children's brushes are used on their own heads.)

Mothers and fathers are always extra gentle when it comes to brushing hair. Ask the children to think of other ways their parents show gentleness toward them.

"...the humble will rejoice in the Lord; ..."   Isaiah 29:19

CUDDLE BUGS

Have children create their own unique Cuddle Bugs using the materials you provide. Cuddle Bugs can ride along in a pocket, hide under a pillow at night, or sit on a favorite shelf, ready to be taken in hand whenever children are in need of feeling reassured by something soft.

Materials:

Colorful craft fur, black or brown yarn, brightly colored felt, scissors, glue

Instructions:

Cut two circles of fur, each about the size of the palm of your hand, for each child. Cut three or four lengths of yarn for each bug, about twice the diameter of the circles. Cut small pieces of felt for eyes. Children with scissor skills can help with the cutting. Place the circles on the table, fur side down. Spread them with glue, and lay the strands of yarn across one circle of each pair so when the other circle is glued on top some of the yarn will hang out on either side to form legs. Glue some bright felt eyes onto the furry bugs. Let dry.

Encourage the children to hold their Cuddle Bugs when they find themselves becoming angry or frustrated and need to remind themselves to be gentle or mild.

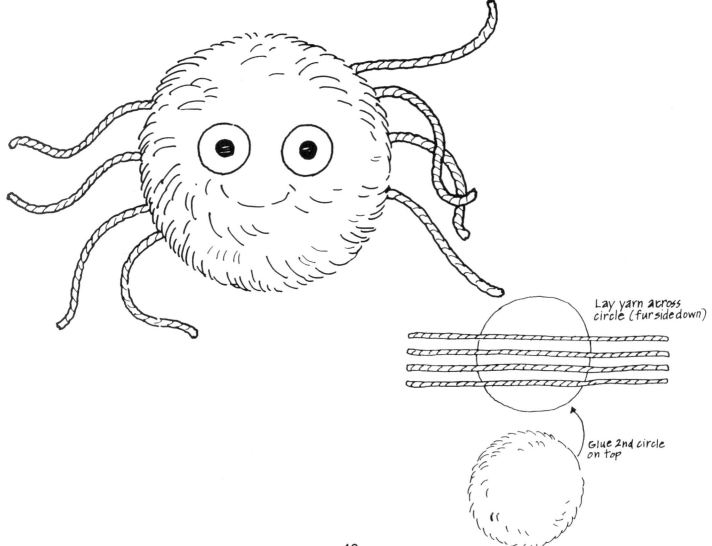

Lay yarn across circle (fur side down)

Glue 2nd circle on top

SS1891

TABLETOP TOTS: LEARNING CENTER SOLUTIONS
SOFT AND SCRATCHY SORTING

Materials:

Soft stuff—small pieces of velvet, cotton, satin, imitation fur, down feathers, etc.; scratchy stuff—small pieces of sandpaper, burlap, rough tree bark, etc.; construction paper, glue, hole punch, yarn

Instructions:

Scatter all the materials on a low table. Invite the children to the table to create a Gentle Touch Collage. First give them a chance to handle all the materials and to separate them into "scratchy" and "soft" piles. Then give them a piece of construction paper and allow them to glue the soft items on it in a random design. Make two holes with a hole punch and string with yarn to hang. Ask the children to think of other soft things that make them feel gentle.

RESOURCES

Ideas for speakers, field trips, projects, books, and other supplementary materials and activities.

Invite a Certified Massage Therapist to talk to the class about the importance of body awareness. The therapist can show the children the benefits of gentle massage in reducing stress and reviving energy. Ask him to show the children a few massage techniques to use on the neck and shoulders so the children might give their parents a special treat at home.

A visiting nurse from a nearby neo-natal unit could give the children a renewed sense of wonder when they realize the gentle care it takes to provide warmth and nurturing for newborn infants. Ask the nurse to bring photos, special supplies, and clothing worn by newborns.

Have a Teddy Bear Story Hour. Invite the children to come wearing their coziest pajamas and bring along their favorite snuggly toy for an hour of story telling. Dim the lights, provide a few healthful snacks, and cozy up to a good book. It's great for children to see each other as soft and gentle snuggle bears.

Try the following books and tapes at circle time to share with your group:

Barret, Joyce Durham
Willie's Not the Hugging Kind
Harper and Row Publishers, 1989.
Willie learns that despite what his friend says, it's not silly at all to want hugs from the people he loves.

Mayer, Mercer
The New Baby
Western Publishing Co., Inc., 1983.
A young child learns it is a different, gentler, kind of play that a new baby enjoys.

Zolotow, Charlotte
Big Sister and Little Sister
Harper and Row Publishers, 1966.
Little Sister finally gets the chance to care for Big Sister; and Big Sister learns to care for Little Sister a bit more gently.

GOODNESS

"...God loves a cheerful giver."   II Corinthians 9:7

GOODNESS POSTER

Children can cut out the picture and color it. They may glue the picture to colored construction paper. Save all the posters to make a fruit of the Spirit banner later. Encourage the children to think of ways their town or community shows its goodness by sharing. Have the children discuss the different ways their families share at home.

"The path of the righteous is like the first gleam of dawn, shining ever brighter till the full light of day." Proverbs 4:18

A GIFT OF GOODNESS: SUN SHINER

Materials:

Crayons, scissors, glue, glitter, colored ribbons or yarn, hole punch, large plastic lid from a margarine tub, copy machine

Instructions:

Make a gift of goodness. First make copies of the pattern, two for each child. Let the children color and cut them out. Brush some glue on the sun's rays and shake on a little glitter for a shiny effect. Cut the colored ribbons or yarn into short strips and have the children glue these to the bottom of the plastic lid. Glue the pictures onto either side of the lid. Make a hole at the top and string with yarn. Give this Sun Shiner decoration to a special friend.

SS1891

"They will celebrate your abundant goodness and joyfully sing of your righteousness."
Psalm 145:7

SHOW SOMEONE JUST HOW YOU CARE!

Sung to: "This Old Man"

Our dear Lord, He helps us,
Helps us to be generous.
With a knick-knack, patty-whack,
be polite and share,
Show someone just how you care!

Our dear Lord, He helps us,
Helps us to be courteous.
With a knick-knack, patty-whack,
open up a door,
Show someone just how you care!

Our dear Lord, He helps us,
Helps us show our cheerfulness.
With a knick-knack, patty-whack,
lend a helping hand,
Show someone just how you care!

Our dear Lord, He gives us,
Gives us love and happiness.
With a knick-knack, patty-whack,
give a pal a hug,
Show someone just how you care!

SS1891

"...the earth is full of the goodness of the Lord."   Psalm 33:5 (KJV)

RECIPE FOR GOODNESS: SHARING SUB

The Sharing Sub reminds us of many of the gifts God has given us: grains for bread, animals for meat, dairy products for cheese, herbs for flavors like mustard, and abundant plant life for fruits and vegetables like tomatoes and lettuce.

Materials:

Paper plates, knives

Ingredients:

Long loaf of French bread, meats, cheeses, spreads, condiments

Instructions:

Make a giant submarine sandwich to share. Have all the children bring something to help build the sandwich such as meats, cheeses or condiments. Let everyone have a hand at layering the ingredients and smearing on the spreads.

As the children make the sandwich, sing the following song:

GOODNESS KNOWS

Sung to: "Row, Row, Row Your Boat"

Good, good, goodness knows. . .
God gives us food and friends!
Merrily, merrily, merrily, merrily,
Such wondrous gifts He sends!

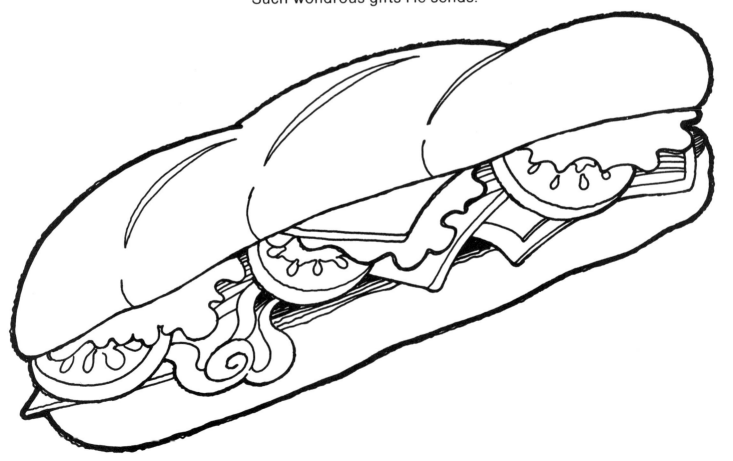

"...the goodness of God endureth continually."   Psalm 52:1 (KJV)

SHOW YOUR STYLE GAME

Christ's goodness comes shining through in little ways, such as when we share a smile with a passerby, pick up a piece of litter or say a cheery thank you.

Materials:

Playing area, ball

Instructions:

Stand in a circle and place the ball in front of one child's feet. Recite the following rhyme together.

Show your heart,	(Put hands over heart.)
Show your smile!	(Poke cheeks while smiling.)
Show your goodness,	(Make a flourishing bow.)
Show your style!	
I show my style by. . .	

The child with the ball gives an example of a way he can show goodness and then kicks the ball gently across the circle to another child who stops it with his feet. That child says, "I show my style by. . ." and gives an example of a way he can show goodness. Continue until all children have had a turn. Remind the children that there are many ways for us to show goodness every day.

"But the fruit of the Spirit is. . .goodness, . . ."   Galatians 5:22

GOOD IN THE MORNIN', GOOD AT NIGHT ACTION VERSE

Be good so early at morning light.   (Fan fingers like the sun's rays.)
Be good 'til late when you say goodnight.   (Rest head on hands to sleep.)
When you brush your teeth,   (Make brushing motions.)
Give thanks for smiles!   (Poke cheeks and smile wide.)
When you drink your milk,   (Tip up a glass.)
Give thanks for cows!   (Say, "Moooo!")

Be good so early at morning light.   (Fan fingers like the sun's rays.)
Be good 'til late when you say goodnight.   (Rest head on hands to sleep.)
When you go to school,   (Shrug.)
Give thanks for. . .recess!   (Pause, then shout, "recess!")
When you're walking home,   (Swing arms back and forth.)
Give thanks for feet!   (Stomp feet.)

Be good so early at morning light.   (Fan fingers like the sun's rays.)
Be good 'til late when you say goodnight.   (Rest head on hands to sleep.)
When dinner is done,   (Bring fork to mouth.)
Give thanks for food!   (Rub tummy.)
When you're tucked in tight,   (Hug self.)
Give thanks for love!   (Blow a kiss.)

Be good so early at morning light.   (Fan fingers like the sun's rays.)
Be good 'til late when you say goodnight.   (Rest head on hands to sleep.)
You're good to me,   (Point to person.)
And I'm good to you.   (Point to self.)
For all your love,   (Place hands over heart.)
I give thanks for you!   (Give the person a hug.)

Note: When working with young ones, master one verse at a time so the children can feel a sense of success. Then move on.

"How great is your goodness, . . ."   Psalm 31:19

ANGEL FOR A DAY

Be an angel for a day! Christ's love and goodness endures because His life was an example for us. Let us make our behavior an example to others.

Materials:

Yellow construction paper, scissors, crayons, glue, glitter, tape or safety pins

Instructions:

Make a simple outline of a star on the yellow paper and have the children cut it out and color it. Brush on glue and sprinkle on some glitter. Pin or tape the star to the child's shoulder as reminder to be good, courteous, and full of love.

Give the children a sandwich bag or small paper bag full of confetti. Let them run about and sprinkle this "angel confetti" as a reminder of their heavenly behavior goals for the day. October 2 is designated the Day of the Guardian Angel, but any day can be! Have children pair up and become Guardian Angels to each other. On this day they can look out for one another by being helpful and mindful of each other's safety.

"I lift up my eyes to the hills—. . ." Psalm 121:1

GOODNESS GLASSES

Materials:

Toilet paper tubes, stickers, vinyl duct tape, yarn, hole punch

Instructions:

Hold two tubes up to the child's eyes like binoculars. Note the space needed between his eyes, and then use vinyl duct tape to secure the tubes together, leaving the needed space between them. Let the child decorate his glasses with stickers. Make a hole on either side and string with yarn so the glasses can be worn around the neck.

Children can use these whimsical tube glasses to remind them to use their eyes to seek and find the goodness of God everyday. When they use their Goodness Glasses they will be reminded to be thankful for all God has given, and in return, to give back to God by showing their goodness to others.

Encourage the use of these fun glasses. You might ask the children to look through their Goodness Glasses at clean-up time to help their eyes spy the messy spots that need cleaning, or before prayer time to take one last look around them and locate that extra special person or thing they wish to give thanks for. Try to spy the special things in life!

 SS1891

". . .see the goodness of the Lord. . ."   Psalm 27:13

TABLETOP TOTS: LEARNING CENTER SOLUTIONS
GOODNESS FLOWER

Children can make a Goodness Flower to take home with them. Each day an adult at home can pull off one of the petals and read the good deed to the child. That day the child will be responsible for performing the deed.

Materials:

White construction paper, five other colors of construction paper, pen, colored markers (matching the paper), scissors, glue

Instructions:

Cut out large petal shapes from each of the five colored pieces of paper (or let children do this if they are able). Outline a circular flower center on the white paper. Using the markers, mark one spot of each of the different colors on the inside edge of the flower center. Choosing appropriate tasks for the age level of the children you are working with, label each petal with a good deed, such as watering the plants, putting toys away, etc. Let the children cut out the white circle for the flower center. Set out the petals. Have the children match the petals by color to the corresponding colored spot on the white center. Add glue and press the petal down in the correct spot. Read the tasks together as a group before the children take their flowers home so they will be prepared to perform their good deeds.

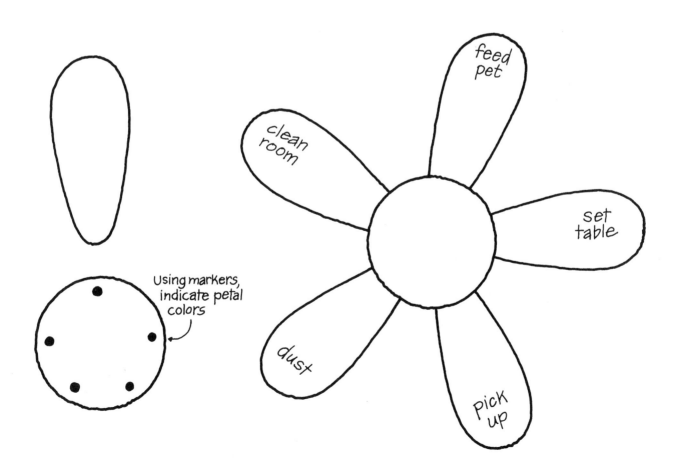

Using markers, indicate petal colors

RESOURCES

Ideas for speakers, field trips, projects, books, tapes, and other supplementary materials and activities.

Invite different types of care givers to talk about their work, or take a trip to a hospital or nursing home to see others who spend their lives sharing God's goodness and caring for the sick or disabled.

If you visit a hospital or nursing home, prepare a short singing program or go laden with handmade gifts and pictures for the elderly. Let the children see that their acts of goodness can really make a difference. Call ahead to find out what kinds of gifts would please the patients most. Before the visit, talk with the children to prepare them for what they will see and hear.

Give children small tasks to let them see that their own acts of goodness and caring are needed and appreciated. Make a schedule that gives a special job to each child on a certain day, such as watering indoor plants, feeding the household or classroom pet, or washing the windows so that others might look out onto a bright world.

Try the following books and tapes at circle time to share with your group:

Curtis, Gavin
Grandma's Baseball
Crown Publishers, Inc., 1990.
Grandma and her grandson open their hearts and learn to understand and appreciate one another.

Hautzig, Deborah
Get Well, Granny Bird
Random House/Children's Television Workshop, 1989.
Big bird shows us that "It's the thought that counts!"

Hayward, Linda
Mine! A Sesame Street Book About Sharing
Random House/Children's Television Workshop, 1988.
Little Bert and Little Ernie learn how to share.

Murphy, Elspeth Campbell
Sometimes I'm Good, Sometimes I'm Bad
Chariot Books, a division of David C. Cook Publishing Co., 1981.
A child feels closer to God, cozier and happier, when he is good.

FAITH

"...'The righteous will live by faith.'"

Galatians 3:11

FAITH POSTER

Children can cut out the picture and color it. They may glue the picture to colored construction paper. Save all the posters to make a fruit of the Spirit banner later. Encourage the children to think of ways they show their faith every day.

A GIFT OF FAITH: CROSS OF MANY COLORS

Materials:

Access to copy machine, black construction paper, crayons, scissors, glue, hole punch, yarn

Instructions:

Make copies of the cross for the children. Let them color it using all the colors mentioned in the poem, and then cut it out. Glue it to the center of the black paper and let dry. Make two holes with a punch and string with yarn to hang. Give this Gift of Faith to a special friend.

GOD'S COLORS

Blue is for the skies above.
Red is Christ's unending love.
White is for God's perfect grace
Green is for the leaves we chase.
Orange is for the delicate flower.
Yellow is for the sun, shining every hour.
These are gifts God gives us;
We have faith He'll watch over us!

SS1891

"You are all sons of God through faith in Christ Jesus," Galatians 3:26

SING HALLE, HALLELUJAH!

Sung to: "Polly Wolly Doodle"

Oh, I went to church, for to see my Lord,

Singin' Halle, Hallelujah all the day.

Oh, my Lord, He is a friend of mine,

Singin' Halle, Hallelujah all the day.

Oh, my Lord, oh, my Lord,

Oh, my Lord, I've come to thee.

For I'm going to Sunday service for to sing You all my praises,

Singin' Halle, Hallelujah all the day.

Oh, my Lord, He has a heart of love,

Singin' Halle, Hallelujah all the day.

And I like to praise my Lord above,

Singin' Halle, Hallelujah all the day.

Oh, my Lord, oh, my Lord,

Oh, my Lord, I've come to thee.

For I'm going to Sunday service for to sing You all my praises,

Singin' Halle, Hallelujah all the day.

SS1891

"Now faith is being sure of what we hope for and certain of what we do not see."

Hebrews 11:1

RECIPE FOR FAITH: BREAD OF LIFE

Making yeast bread is a great way to introduce children to the many mysteries of life. We can't always see things happen, but we know they do. Every spring, flowers bloom overnight and caterpillars miraculously become butterflies. A baby grows in a mother's womb—we can't see it, but we have faith that it is happening. And somehow we grow taller without even noticing it!

Let children do all the kneading. Make sure they notice the shape and size of the bread before they cover it so that they can see how it has risen. After baking, break bread together in a special way. Perhaps you could drink juice from special "company" glasses just this once, or decorate paper cups especially for the occasion.

Materials:

Rolling pin, cutting board, two loaf pans

Ingredients:

2 cups of very warm water, 2 envelopes dry yeast, 2 Tbs. sugar, 1 tsp. salt, 1/4 cup salad oil, 6 to 6 1/2 cups all-purpose flour

Instructions:

Dissolve the yeast in warm water. Stir in the sugar, salt, oil, and half the flour. Beat until smooth. Mix in remaining flour, enough to make dough easy to handle and not too sticky. Knead dough on floured board for about 10 minutes, until smooth and elastic. Brush top with salad oil, cover, and let rise in a warm place for about 45 minutes.

Punch down dough with fist, and divide in half. Roll each half into a rectangle. Beginning at the short side, form dough into loaves. Seal ends by pressing down. Fold ends under, and then place seam side down in greased loaf pans. Brush loaves with salad oil. Let rise for another hour until almost double. Heat oven to 400 degrees. Bake about 35 minutes. (Loaves will have a hollow sound when tapped.)

SS1891

" 'Because you have seen me, you have believed; blessed are those who have not seen and yet have believed.' "

John 20:29

PIN YOUR FAITH IN JESUS GAME

Materials:

Bulletin board; black, white, and yellow construction paper; empty round oats box; crayons; long push pins; glue; X-acto knife; blindfold; copy machine

Instructions:

Make a copy of the Jesus pattern for each child. Have each child cut out and color his own Jesus. While the children are coloring, create the bulletin board pictured. Place on a few white puffy clouds and a glowing yellow sun. Cut the oats box in half, and cover with the black paper. Tack the box onto the board with the lid (as the stone) off to one side. Have one child approach the board with his Jesus pattern. Place the pattern in the tomb, and then blindfold the child. Spin him once or twice, and then have him approach the board and hunt for the tomb. When he finds it, have him reach inside for his resurrected Jesus. Now he can hold it to the board in the place he thinks is appropriate. Tack it on for him. Remove the blindfold and the next child plays. After everyone has played, let the children move their patterns and place them anywhere they wish.

"so that Christ may dwell in your hearts through faith. And I pray that you, being rooted and established in love, . . .may have power. . .grasp. . .the love of Christ, . . ."

Ephesians 3:17, 18

FAITH THAT GOD'S IN ME ACTION VERSE

This is my body, fingers and toes,
(Hold arms out, wiggle fingers, toes.)

Big round eyes, one little nose.
(Point to eyes, then nose.)

This is my body, where is my soul?
(Hold arms out, then shrug.)

Deep in my heart where no one sees,
(Cross hands over heart, wag finger.)

But there I know my God loves me!
(Hug self.)

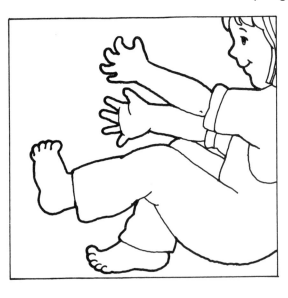

SS1891

"We live by faith, not by sight."   II Corinthians 5:7

WALK WITH TRUST

Materials:

Blindfold, safe grassy outdoor area or an indoor area free of any obstacles

Instructions:

Have fun with this simple exercise that reminds children that it sometimes takes great faith to trust in frightening situations. Simply take turns letting the children be blindfolded and led on a short walk. Always walk slowly, talk softly, and keep physical contact at all times. Take a Walk with Trust *only* when *led by adults* and *never* when a child verbalizes or demonstrates any hesitancy.

Let the children stop to handle the bushes or leaves they brush against. Ask them to visualize where they are. Children wary of a blindfold may wish to simply close their eyes. Or you might put a few objects in a paper bag, and let children close their eyes and then handle them, guessing what they might be.

Talk about people with handicaps such as blindness, hearing loss, or loss of mobility. In certain situations, these people may have to place their trust in other people or in their other senses. Have the children talk about times they felt dependent on others and when they needed to feel trusting.

SS1891

"let us draw near to God with a sincere heart in full assurance of faith, . . ."

Hebrews 10:22

POCKETFUL OF PRAYERS

Materials:

White paper plates, colorful felt, hole punch, thick hair yarn, tape, stapler, crayons, stickers

Instructions:

Wrap a small piece of tape around one end of a length of yarn. Cut half circles of felt, exactly half the size of the paper plates. Line up the round edges of the felt and plate and punch holes all around the edge. Show the children how to take the taped end of the yarn and poke it in and out to lace the two pieces together. Staple the ends to the back side of the plate. If necessary, add a few more staples to help secure the pocket. Let the children decorate the exposed portions of the plate with crayons and stickers. They may want to draw a little cross.

Children can tack their Pocketful of Prayers on a wall near their bed. Each day they can draw a small picture of a special concern about which they can pray. At night they can slip the picture into the pocket.

TABLETOP TOTS: LEARNING CENTER SOLUTIONS
CIRCLE OF TRUST

Focus on fostering trust between children and adults. When children glue their pictures to the center of the Trust Circle, talk about the importance of going to people within their circle for help. Children must learn to be trusting yet at the same time develop caution and safety awareness. Discuss not talking to strangers and any other safety tips they might have learned from their parents.

Materials:

Large piece of white paper; photo of child, parents, and other significant adults in the child's life; scissors; glue; crayons

Instructions:

Cut a very large circle from the white paper. Let the children glue photos of themselves to the center of the white paper. They may wish to frame them by drawing fancy borders around them with the crayons. Now they may glue the pictures of adult family members on around the outside edge of the circle. Next they can color and cut out pictures of community helpers and glue these on, too.

RESOURCES

Ideas for speakers, field trips, projects, books, and other supplementary materials and activities.

Invite a Christian professional, missionary, or volunteer to talk about how he shares his faith with others. Ask him to give personal, everyday examples of how he relies on his faith, or how he has seen others' faith bring them through a tough time. Ask him to give the children ideas on how they might reaffirm their own faith.

Try the following books and tapes at circle time to share with your group:

Anderson, Debby
Jesus Loves Me
Chariot Books, a division of David C. Cook Publishing Co., 1988.
A great board book for toddlers.

Jefferson, Graham
Would You Like to Know Jesus?
Chariot Books, a division of David C. Cook Publishing Co., 1988.
Children learn that they can be friends with Jesus.

Murphy, Elspeth Campbell
Sometimes I Get Mad
Chariot Books, a division of David C. Cook Publishing Co., 1981.
Kids will really relate to this child.

Tangvald, Christine Harder
A Child's Book of Prayers
Chariot Books, a division of David C. Cook Publishing Co., 1987.
This is a book of short prayers just for kids.

Tangvald, Christine Harder
I Can Talk to God
Chariot Books, a division of David C. Cook Publishing Co., 1985.
Children learn that it is easy to share their thoughts with God.

PATIENCE

"...bring forth fruit with patience."   Luke 8:15 (KJV)

PATIENCE POSTER

Children can cut out the picture and color it. Glue the picture to colored construction paper. Save all the posters to make a fruit of the Spirit banner later. Encourage the children to think of some favorite things they must wait for patiently.

"...we consider blessed those who have persevered...."   James 5:11

A GIFT OF PATIENCE: PATIENCE PICTURE PUZZLES

Create a personal gift that helps develop patience and is full of fun.

Materials:

A large photograph of each child or his family or any picture he chooses, clear Con-Tact paper, colored construction paper, glue, scissors, envelopes, crayons

Instructions:

First have the children glue the photos onto squares of colored construction paper. Cover the photos front and back with Con-Tact paper. Cut the photos into several pieces. Allow the children to practice assembling the photos a few times to recreate the picture. Scribble colorful messages on the envelopes, slip the pieces inside, and give to a friend or family member.

Starting a beginner's jigsaw puzzle at home or in the classroom is a perfect group activity that reinforces the virtues of patience. Many puzzles are available with twenty-five or fewer large pieces. Ask the children if anyone they know has ever completed a puzzle with hundreds of tiny pieces. Ask them if they can recall what the puzzle pictured.

To Mom
Some pieces
of love.
Love,
Patrick

SS1091

". . .Here is the patience and the faith of the saints."   Revelation 13:10 (KJV)

PATIENCE, PATIENCE, I NEED YOU

Sung to: "Twinkle, Twinkle, Little Star"

Patience, patience, I need you.
How I wonder what to do.
Sit right down and twiddle my thumbs,
Tap my toe or sit and hum.
Patience, patience, I need you.
How I wonder what to do.

For the Lord I will be strong,
Even if the wait is long.
With some patience I'll be bright.
I won't grumble, I won't fight.
Patience, patience, I need you.
Now I know just what to do.

        SS1891

"But if we hope for what we do not yet have, we wait for it patiently."   Romans 8:25

RECIPES FOR PATIENCE

LEMONADE

Materials:

Manual juicer, knife

Ingredients:

3 cups water, lemons to make 1 cup lemon juice, 1/2 cup sugar

Instructions:

Slice lemons in half and let everyone have a try at juicing them by hand. Talk about what it will take to make the lemonade: a little elbow grease, a little sugar, and a little time. Explain to the children that with time and hard work, good things can come. Makes about 5 servings of 3/4 cup each.

FRUIT CUBES

Materials:

One or two ice cube trays, Popsicle sticks, measuring cups

Ingredients:

Orange, apple, grape and/or cherry juices

Instructions:

Provide spouted measuring cups for the juices and pour a little into each. Allow the children to fill each square of the ice cube trays with a different juice. Lean a Popsicle stick into each square and freeze. Remember: A watched fridge never freezes!

Fruit cube

SS18

"...let us run with patience the race that is set before us," Hebrews 12:1 (KJV)

CHEERIOS PATIENCE RACE

Materials:

Clay, dry Cheerios or other O-shaped cereal, toothpicks

Instructions:

Divide into teams if you wish, or one group can play noncompetitively. Remind the children that careful work demands patience and concentration. Let them try this relay race to show them how important it is to slow down and think clearly when trying to complete a task.

On a low table put one or two clumps of clay and a bowl of Cheerios. As each child runs a certain distance to the table, poke a toothpick into the clay. Have the child carefully place four Cheerios onto the toothpick and then run back. IMPORTANT: Avoid the possibility of a child falling onto the toothpick in her rush to get to the table. *Always* remove the toothpick each time, and then replace it *only* after the child has come to a full stop at the table.

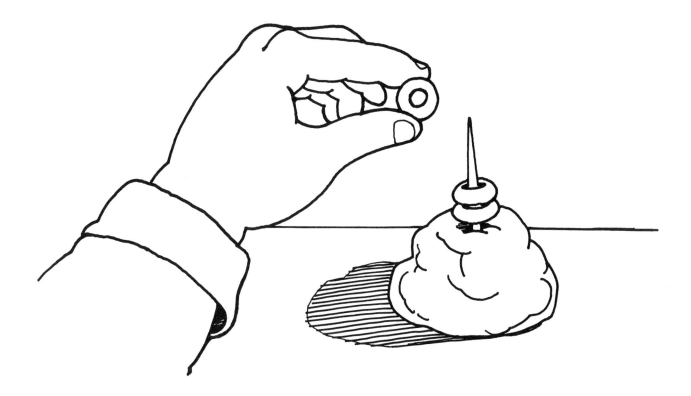

SS1891

"...follow after...patience,..."   I Timothy 6:11 (KJV)

WHEN THINGS GO WRONG ACTION VERSE

When things go wrong,
When you stub your toe,
(Stub toe into carpet and wince.)

You gotta have patience,
(Clap, Clap.) Don't you know!

When things go wrong,
When you're feeling low,
(Frown with drooped shoulders.)

You gotta have patience,
(Clap, Clap.) Don't you know!

So stand up straight,
(Stand up straight and tall.)

Just make a happy face!
(Pass hand over face, reveal a smile.)

You gotta have patience,
(Clap, Clap.) For heaven's sake!

SS1891

PATIENCE POTS

Materials:

Fast growing seeds (like nasturtium or radish), paper cups, potting soil, Popsicle sticks, marking pens, stickers

Instructions:

Poke holes in the bottom of paper cups for drainage, fill with soil and bury seeds to the depth specified on the packages. Water as directed and wait patiently for signs of new life to appear. Make cheerful plant sticks by marking on the Popsicle sticks or pressing on stickers. Place these carefully into Patience Pots.

Reinforce patience with these simple activities:

Construct a house of cards or of dominoes. Younger children can stack blocks carefully one on top of another for a super skyscraper.

* * * * *

Purchase a rock-growing kit at your local toy store for some magical fun. "Pickup Sticks" and "Don't Spill the Beans" are other common games of patience.

"And patience, experience; and experience, hope:" Romans 5:4 (KJV)

LITTLE PIGGY'S BRICK HOUSE

The three little pigs learned from experience that it takes hard work and patience to build something of lasting value.

Materials:

Small squares of cardboard, sugar cubes, glue

Instructions:

Arrange materials and allow the children to build their own sturdy houses. Have them glue a solid foundation of cubes to the cardboard then build up from there. Younger children might enjoy listening to *The Three Little Pigs* or an audio tape of the story as they work. Ask the children to give examples of what they have "learned from experience." They might think of things that are learned best by trial and error, like riding a bike or jumping rope.

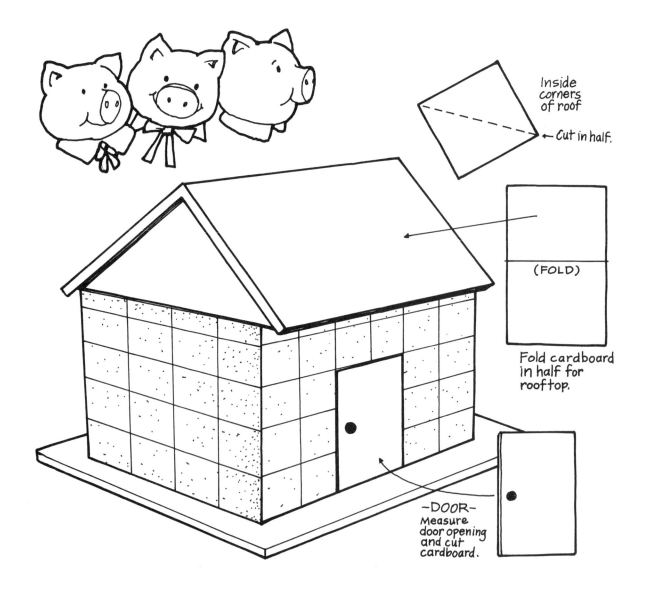

Inside corners of roof
←Cut in half.

(FOLD)

Fold cardboard in half for rooftop.

—DOOR—
Measure door opening and cut cardboard.

SS1891

"Be patient, then, brothers, until the Lord's coming. . . ." James 5:7

TABLETOP TOTS: LEARNING CENTER SOLUTIONS
BEANS IN A BOTTLE

Materials:

A very large mason jar or other clear crock, muffin tins, one- or three-minute sand timers, dried beans and peas (in varying types and sizes to fill the jar and make it colorful and interesting looking)

Instructions:

Mix the peas and beans and fill the jar. Tape one different pea or bean to each cup of the sectioned muffin tins. Set out the jar, the muffin tins, and the timers on a low table. The child should take a timer, turn it over, and reach inside the jar for a handful of beans. He may begin sorting the peas and beans, placing each one in its proper section of the muffin tin. When all the sand has run through the timer, the task is done and another child has a turn.

Try this: Have a Guess the Number of Beans Contest. Fill a small jar with beans and allow the children to guess the number of beans in the jar. Offer a small prize to the closest guess. Ask the children to think of other situations when timers or clocks help us to wait and remind us to be patient.

Shining Star Publications, Copyright © 1991, A division of Good Apple   SS1891

RESOURCES

Ideas for speakers, field trips, projects, books, tapes, and other supplementary materials and activities.

Invite a skilled craftsman like a potter or weaver to the class to speak about his work and demonstrate the patience it takes to create a work of art. Perhaps this visit could be combined with some clay molding or simple yarn weaving done by the children.

Try the following books and tapes at circle time to share with your group:

Berenstain, Stan and Jan
The Berenstain Bears and the Big Road Race
Random House, Inc., 1987.
A Berenstain Bears version of the Tortoise and the Hare and the value of the old adage "slow and steady wins the race."

Collins, Pat Lowery
Taking Care of Tucker
G. P. Putnam's Sons, 1989.
Tucker *finally* comes to appreciate Millie's care.

Ingoglia, Gina
Saggy Baggy Elephant, No Place for Me
Western Publishing Co., Inc., 1989.
Just when he is about to become discouraged, Saggy finds his place in the circus and realizes the value of patience.

Salzman, Yuri
The Three Little Pigs
Western Publishing Co., Inc., 1988.
A classic which is still timely.

Steig, William
Spinky Sulks
Farrar, Straus, and Giroux, 1988.
Spinky's family shows great restraint and patience as they let him sulk his days away until he comes to terms with his emotions.

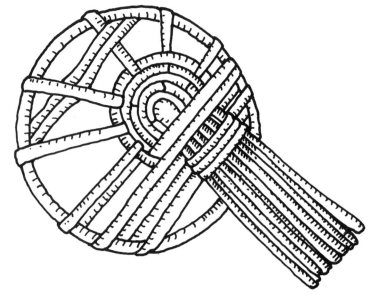

KINDNESS

"...I will show kindness..."   II Samuel 10:2

KINDNESS POSTER

Children can cut out the picture and color it. Glue the picture to colored construction paper. Save all the posters to make a fruit of the Spirit banner later. Encourage the children to think of other animals that might benefit from their kindness. What could they do for a dog? Take him for a walk. A cat? Scratch behind his ears, and so on.

SS1891

". . .do show kindness this day. . ." II Samuel 3:8 (KJV)

A GIFT OF KINDNESS: TWEETY BIRD TREAT

Children can readily see that their acts of kindness are appreciated, especially when bestowed upon the gentle creatures of God's kingdom. Help them to construct this simple bird treat, and then let them discover how their own kindness gives back the pleasure of bird watching!

Materials:

Large, extra thick unsalted pretzels; peanut butter; plastic knife; birdseed; bowl

Instructions:

Cover the area with newspaper. Allow the children to smear the pretzels liberally with peanut butter, front and back. Pour the birdseed into a bowl. Dip the pretzels into the birdseed to coat both sides. Hang this little bird treat over a twig or tree branch near a window and watch the tweety birds feast!

". . .'I tell you the truth, whatever you did for the one of the least of these brothers of mine, you did for me.' "

Matthew 25:40

SOMEONE NEEDS KINDNESS AND CARE

Sung to: "Oh, Dear, What Can the Matter Be?"

Oh, dear, what can the matter be?
Oh, dear, what can the matter be?
Oh, dear, what can the matter be?
Someone needs kindness and care.

Show them you love them and care for them deeply,
Say a kind word, oh, I'm sure it will please them.
Give them a hug or a kiss or a handshake,
To cheer up an unhappy face.

Oh, dear, what can the matter be?
Oh, dear, what can the matter be?
Oh, dear, what can the matter be?
Someone needs kindness and care.

Write them a letter or pick them some flowers,
Draw them a picture or just say "I love you."
Give them a hug or a kiss or a handshake
To cheer up an unhappy face.

". . .according to the kindness that I have done unto thee, thou shalt do unto me, . . ."

Genesis 21:23 (KJV)

RECIPE FOR KINDNESS: BLUEBERRY MUFFINS IN A BASKET

Let the children help mix the batter and then arrange their own gift baskets. Baskets can be delivered to a nursing home, a homeless meals center, a fire station, or other community helper station.

Materials:

Plastic strawberry baskets, paper, crayons, colored tissue paper, paper muffin cups, muffin pans

Ingredients:

1/2 cup milk, 1 egg, 1/4 cup salad oil, 1 1/2 cups all-purpose flour, 1/2 cup sugar, 1/2 tsp. salt, 2 tsp. baking powder, 1 can blueberries

Instructions:

Preheat oven to 400 degrees. Put paper muffin cups in muffin pans. Beat eggs, then stir in remaining ingredients until flour is moistened. Batter will be slightly lumpy. Drain blueberries and fold into batter. Fill muffin cups 2/3 full. Bake 20 to 25 minutes. While muffins cool, have children create a one-of-a-kind picture or poem. Next, give them each a sheet of tissue paper and have them line a strawberry basket. Tuck in muffins and their personal greetings, and this recipe for kindness is ready to go!

Mrs. Dooley, you're so sweet, I thought you'd like this special treat ♡ Love, Sarah

SS1891

"...when all goes well with you, remember me and show me kindness; ..."

Genesis 40:14

KINDNESS CAROUSEL GAME

Materials:

Seven or more chairs, source of music, access to copier, tape, crayons (optional)

Instructions:

Set up the chairs in a row, but be sure to have one for each child. Make two copies of the pictures, three if playing with a large group. Let the children color the pictures. Tape one picture from the first set on each chair and place the other set in a bag. Start the music, and have the children circle the chairs. When the music stops, the children should sit down on the chairs. The teacher then pulls one picture out of the bag. The child whose picture on his chair matches the picture pulled from the bag now stands and gives an example of an act of kindness that might be especially appropriate for the day shown in the picture. Remind them that their ideas can be put to use any day!

"...for ye showed kindness to all the children..." I Samuel 15:6 (KJV)

KINDS OF KINDNESS ACTION VERSE

Children will have fun acting out this verse in pairs. Make paper airplanes to use as props. Then practice a little and perform for parents or friends.

You can make someone feel better
(Shake hands with partner.)

When you show it with a smile.
(Point to cheeks and smile.)

You can put it in a letter
(Pretend to write.)

And send it 'cross the miles.
(Throw paper airplanes.)

You can show it with some kisses.
(Blow kisses.)

You can show it with a squeeze.
(Give partner a hug.)

You can show it with good wishes.
(Give partner a pat on back.)

You can show it saying "please."
(Fold hands, say please.)

Kindness comes around again.
(Turn around.)

Just show some now and then!
(Join hands and walk away.)

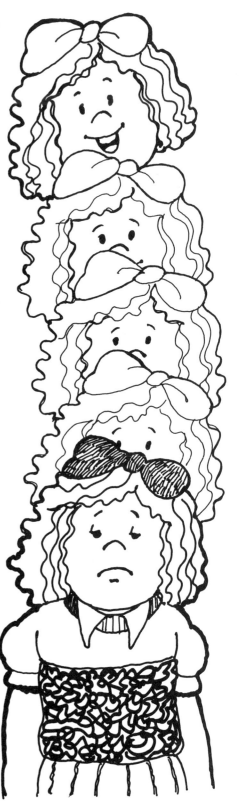

SS1891

"For I was hungry and you gave me something to eat, . . ."   Matthew 25:35

PENNY PINCHERS

It is easy to show kindness when you receive the immediate satisfaction of an appreciative hug or thank you. It may be a bit harder when you never actually see the fruit of your kind labors. Remind the children that there are plenty of people who can benefit from our kindness, even though we do not know them and may never see them. Start this Penny Pinchers program to teach children that every little bit really does help!

Materials:

Plastic margarine tub with lid, crayons, glue, X-acto knife, access to copier

Instructions:

Make copies of the penny pattern. Have children color the pattern and cut it out. Glue the penny onto the lid. Press on the lid and carefully make a slice through the marked slot. Encourage the children to collect any extra pennies and deposit them in the Penny Pincher, especially those pennies found on the ground! After several weeks of saving, collect the Penny Pinchers and deliver them to charity.

"When the Lord saw her, his heart went out to her. . ."   Luke 7:13

BAND-AID BEST WISHES: GET WELL CARD

Materials:

Sheets of red and white paper, scissors, glue, markers, Band-Aids

Instructions:

Cut out a red heart shape, or let children do this if they are able. Show the children how to fold the white sheet of paper in half. Have them glue the red heart to the outside of the card. Show them how to use markers to add arms, legs, and a head to create a big-hearted stick figure. Now they can open and press a Band-Aid across the heart to symbolize a wish for quick healing. Sign, "with love," and tuck this Get Well Card away until some cheery good wishes are needed.

TABLETOP TOTS: LEARNING CENTER SOLUTIONS
GARDENING COUNTING GAME

We can show our kindness and respect for God's gifts in many ways, such as caring for plants. This tabletop game reminds children that much depends upon their kindness and reinforces their counting skills as well.

Materials:

Long strip of white paper, watering can with open top children can reach into, colored paper, medium-sized Styrofoam ball, fringed cocktail picks, crayons and markers or flower stickers, plastic or paper cup, silk or plastic flower buds (often used on bridal favors)

Instructions:

Mark the long strip into twelve sections and place a flower sticker on each one or draw flowers in to make a garden path. Mark a dozen small pieces of paper each with a number from one to six. Place in the can. Place the garden path between the watering can and the cup. Rest the Styrofoam ball in the cup. Put the fringed picks in a bowl. Flowers are markers. Children take turns pulling numbered papers from the can, counting that number of spaces, and placing their markers on the correct squares. Return the paper to the can and play continues. The first person to reach the flower bulb may poke in a fringed flower petal! Continue until all players reach the bulb and the flower is in full bloom. Play can be repeated, adding more and more petals.

RESOURCES

Ideas for speakers, field trips, projects, books, tapes, and other supplementary materials and activities.

Invite a veterinarian to speak about her work, and ask her to describe the special needs of different types of pets. The veterinarian may be able to offer the children specific suggestions in showing appropriate acts of kindness for their particular pets.

Take a field trip to your local ASPCA or animal shelter. Many communities have educational outreach programs that will bring speakers into the classroom. Check your local yellow pages.

Try the following books and tapes at circle time to share with your group:

Garis, Howard R.
Uncle Wiggly to the Rescue
See chapter titled, "Uncle Wiggly and the Butterfly."
Platt and Munk, Publisher, 1988.
Uncle Wiggly shows great kindness when he comes to the rescue of a wounded butterfly. When he falls ill, his kindness is returned in a special way.

Murphy, Elspeth Campbell
God Cares When I'm Feeling Mean
Chariot Books, a division of David C. Cook Publishing, Co., 1984.
God loves children even when they're not behaving.

Pederson, Judy
The Tiny Patient
Alfred A. Knopf, Inc., 1989.
A little girl's kindness pays off when she rescues and revives a sick bird.

Wild, Margaret
Mr. Nick's Knitting
Harcourt Brace Jovanovich, 1989.
A touching story about the special relationship between Mr. Nick and his friend and how he shows kindness, as only he can, when she falls ill.

SS1891

SELF-CONTROL

". . .the fruit of the Spirit is. . .self-control."

Galatians 5:22, 23

SELF-CONTROL POSTER

Children can cut out the poster and color it. Glue the picture to colored construction paper. Save all the posters to make a fruit of the Spirit banner later. Encourage the children to think of certain times when they may need to remember their manners and show a little self-control.

SS1891

"...I am prudent:..."   Isaiah 10:13 (KJV)

A GIFT OF SELF-CONTROL: INCREDIBLE EDIBLE NECKLACE OF GOOD THOUGHTS

This gift will really be appreciated when the receiver realizes what concentration, care, and genuine good thoughts went into its making.

Materials:

Cheerios or other O-shaped cereal, Froot Loops or other colored O-shaped cereal, lengths of yarn, tape, bowls

Instructions:

Place the Cheerios in a large bowl and the Froot Loops in a separate bowl. Take a short piece of tape and wind it tightly around one end of the yarn to create a needle of sorts. Knot the other end several times so the cereal pieces will not slide off. Now the children can make edible necklaces for people they love. String on several plain Cheerios and then add one Froot Loop. Keep stringing several plain Cheerios, adding just one Froot Loop now and then. Each time they add a Froot Loop, have the children say a little prayer to the Lord. They may ask for special blessings, good health, and happiness for the person of whom they are thinking. Or the children may simply give a thought of thanks that that person is a part of their lives. The necklaces need not be filled in all the way around. A tasty, edible necklace like this, laced with bits of colorful good thoughts, will surely be appreciated.

"Watch and pray so that you will not fall into temptation. . . ."   Matthew 26:41

RECIPE FOR SELF-CONTROL: LITTLE CORN POPPERS

Materials:

Stove, pan, napkins, large bowl

Ingredients:

Popping corn, butter and salt if desired

Instructions:

Depending upon the size of the group, let the children measure out a certain amount of corn and then pour it into the pan.

Have the children lie on the floor within earshot of the popcorn and pretend to be kernels of corn. Tell them they must concentrate and try to control their movements, keeping their mouths and bodies still, just like the kernels of corn in the bottom of the pan. Begin the exercise well before the corn starts to pop, and then gradually, as little pops are heard, allow the children to twitch and pop as the corn does, popping and jumping harder and faster as the corn begins to go wild in the pan. When the popping stops, have the children settle down and become still again.

CORN POP RAP

After snacking on the popcorn for a while, place a large bowl on the floor and sit around it in a circle. Talk about all the different times it might be difficult for children to control their body movements or excitement. Have them name some times and places when they must try especially hard to be quiet and attentive. Before sharing their thoughts, each child must hold up a piece of popped corn. When you point to him, he may place the corn in the bowl. Only then may he speak. Everyone else remains quiet to listen.

                                    SS1891

"A gentle answer turns away wrath, but a harsh word stirs up anger."   Proverbs 15:1

SCREAM MACHINE

Children will do much better in containing their emotional outbursts if they know that there are times when loud, rambunctious behavior is allowed and accepted.

Materials:

Cardboard refrigerator box or large packing crate, bright paints, brushes, butcher paper, scissors, staple gun

Instructions:

Create a Scream Machine children can use to let off some steam. Find an old refrigerator box or packing crate and gather up some bright paints. Allow the children to go wild decorating their Scream Machine. You can paint directly on the cardboard, or cover a wooden packing crate with paper and then paint. Stand the box out on the porch or in the yard. When the children are feeling frustrated, angry, or especially wild and crazy, they can come to you quietly and ask to enter the Scream Machine. Once inside they may yell and stomp as loudly as they like. But when they come out, they must be self-controlled and considerate again.

SS1891

"and to knowledge, self-control; and to self-control, perseverance; and to perseverance, godliness;"

II Peter 1:6

SQUIRMY WORMS ACTION VERSE

When you're wigglin' like a worm,
(Wiggle.)

Say, "Excuse me."
(Give a bow or curtsy.)

Show some self-control!
(Stand up straight and still.)

When you really have to squirm,
(Squirm around.)

Say, "Excuse me."
(Give a bow or curtsy.)

Show some self-control!
(Stand up straight and still.)

When you're pokin' and a pushin',
(Poke at nose, pretend to push.)

Say, "Excuse me."
(Give a bow or curtsy.)

Show some self-control!
(Stand up straight and still.)

When you're itchin' and a twitchin',
(Itch body and twitch.)

Say, "Excuse me."
(Give a bow or curtsy.)

Show some self-control!
(Stand up straight and still.)

SS1891

"Do not defile the land where you live. . ."   Numbers 35:34

THE CAN MAN

Start a simple recycling project and help the young children learn that just a little effort and self-control can help avoid waste and pollution.

Materials:

Old plastic or metal trash can, a long sheet of butcher paper or newsprint paper, paints or markers, heavy vinyl duct tape

Instructions:

Cut the roll of paper to fit around the can and secure with the tape. Let children decorate the can with the figure of a man and any other designs they choose. Label it, "The Can Man" and encourage the children to fill it to the brim with aluminum cans. The same process can be used to create a "Newspaper Nellie" recycling bin. Cut out a dress shape from the newspaper and paste on the covered can, decorate, and start tossing in the old newsprint.

Ask the children to save useful items at home such as milk cartons, plastic tubs, paper towel tubes, and scraps of fabric and ribbon. These can all be used to create unique arts and crafts projects.

". . .self-control. Against such there is no law." Galatians 5:23

TABLETOP TOTS: LEARNING CENTER SOLUTIONS

Children will try their hardest to play along with you in this exercise using these colorful and tasty materials. Reward them afterward for a job well done by allowing them to eat their materials!

TASTY TEST OF SELF-CONTROL

Materials:

Large bag of M & M's or other multicolored snack candy or cereal, paper towels

Instructions:

Give the children each a pile of snacks, an equal number in each pile. Let them start by sorting them by color. Next, depending upon the age of the group, call out different numbers and have the children set out that many snack pieces. Or call out a problem, "2 + 4" and let the children set out the numbers as you call them and then count to get the answer.

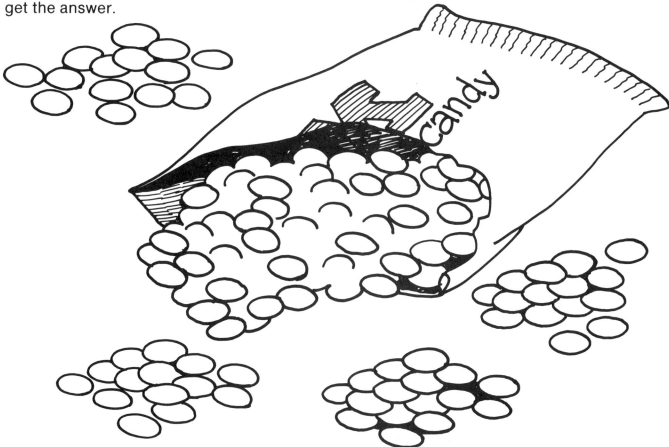

Ask the children to tell you what helps them to keep their minds on a task. What distracts them? Remind them that God has given them strength to meet challenges, and they may call on His help whenever they feel their strength faltering. Little tricks like patting oneself on the back and saying "You can do it!" right out loud are good for bolstering spirits and encouraging oneself to go on.

RESOURCES

Ideas for speakers, field trips, projects, books, tapes, and other supplementary materials and activities.

Invite a juggler or gymnast to demonstrate his skills. Allow him to talk with the children about the great amount of self-control that is needed to perform such physical feats. Remind the children that it always takes practice to achieve success.

To illustrate the power of practice, have the children try to draw a picture or write their names with the hand not usually used. They will laugh when they see the results, but will realize what can happen with practice.

Set up a simple game. Have the children kneel on a chair, lean over the back of it, and try to drop clothespins into a bottle placed on the floor. (Use a wide-mouthed jar for very young ones.) They can practice several times a day, even playing the game at home. They may find that over a week's time they have improved greatly.

Try the following books and tapes at circle time to share with your group:

Berenstain, Stan and Jan
The Berenstain Bears and Too Much Junk Food
Random House, Inc., 1985.
Papa Bear and the kids learn that it takes a little self-control to keep good eating habits under control.

CoCo, Eugene Bradley
Baby Brown Bear's Big Bellyache
Western Publishing Co., Inc., 1989.
Bear forgets his promise, eats the whole jar of honey, and regrets it later.

Hockerman, Barbara
The Potluck Supper
Victor Books, a division of SP Publications, Inc., 1988.
Little Mouse gets greedy in the face of a giant cheese.

Scarry, Richard
Naughty Bunny
Western Publishing Co., Inc., 1989.
Children will see themselves in this funny book about Naughty Bunny who tries very hard to be good—and finally succeeds.

Shining Star Publications, Copyright © 1991, A division of Good Apple   SS1891